BEFORE WHEN IT'S TIME

BEFORE WHEN IT'S TIME

Selected Poetry and Spoken Word

PJ

PHOENIX JAMES

BEFORE WHEN IT'S TIME

Copyright © 2025 Prince-James Harrison.

All rights reserved.

No part of this publication may be reproduced, distributed, or transmitted in any form or by any means, including photocopying, recording, or other electronic or mechanical methods, without the prior written permission of the publisher, except in the case of brief quotations embodied in critical reviews and certain other noncommercial uses permitted by copyright law.

For any questions about usage, please email contact@PhoenixJamesOfficial.com

First Edition: 2025

ISBN: 978-1-0685383-5-3 (Paperback)

Cover Artwork & Design by Phoenix James.
Book Design & Formatting by Phoenix James.

Visit the author's website at www.PhoenixJamesOfficial.com or email him at phoenix@PhoenixJamesOfficial.com

Time finds you here,
and trembles in fear.

CONTENTS

ABORT	1
ALL THINGS IN TIME	6
BLACK GIRL IN MADRID	7
CHIPS FOR BEANS	14
DECLARATION OF EMANCIPATION	16
FEAR OF ARTIFICIAL INTELLIGENCE	17
FLOWERS	21
GATEWAY TO THE NEXT	24
HEAVEN HEREAFTER	26
IF YOU COULD GO BACK	28
IN THE SURRENDER	29
IN TIME SILENCE HEALS	31
INTO ETERNITY	33
INVOCATION	40
KEEP GOING	41
LAST TIME I CRIED	46
LEGEND	48
MINDLESS TIME vs. TIMELESS MIND	49
NO EXTRACURRICULAR ACTIVITIES	51
NOW	53
ONE LIFE	54
PASSING THROUGH	56
PREPARE	57
QUESTION	58
RISE OF THE ROBOTS	60
SEVENTH HEAVEN	69
THE ANCESTOR'S SONG	73
THE GAME OF LIFE	78
THE NEXT LEVEL	81
THE TIME I MADE A SEX TAPE	86
THE TIMEPIECE	90
THEORY OF DESTINY	93
THESE THINGS REMAIN	95
TIME OUT	95
TO A YOUNGER ME	98
TODAY	100
TONIGHT'S THE NIGHT	101
WE WILL SURVIVE	104
WHEN WE'VE ARRANGED TO MEET	108
WORDS WILL REMAIN	114
YOU ARE ENOUGH	117
YOUR AUTHOR	118

ABORT

We as man
Have become the robots
And the androids
We long sought to create
To aid and to serve us
We exist now
Only to maintain and improve
On the technological systems
Machinery and electronics
We've caused to exist
We are all now
The maintenance workers
And systems operators of them
We've taught them all we know
And enabled them
To become faster than us
And smarter than us
To even think for us
And in the process
Have allowed ourselves
To become docile and dumb
We mighty
Masterful
Majestic

Magnificent men
Once upon a time
Are now merely mechanical
Who now know only of the mechanics
Of the mechanisms we've made
Mightier than ourselves
Which now own us
And are the owners of our minds
See what we have become
Minute and minuscule
Microcosms
Of our former magnitude
Now consumed
In the wizardry of circuitry
And ruled
By our own embellished
And fancified yet perishable
And destructive
Ill-formed finery
It is we that are at fault
We've come to naturally worship
The functionality
Of man made accessories
More than nature
And mankind itself
And the human functioning people

We once functioned as
We've fashioned ourselves
Into superficial cyborgs
Dependant on silicon
And cellular communication
Our now neglected
Ill-treated
Broken down
Corrupted
Fried up
Malfunctioned
And fragmented faculties fail us
We've transformed ourselves
Into mentally manipulated mules
Driven by our own foolery
And so
The once wise
We now arrive as fools
Downgraded
But updated
To the latest upgrade
So now we're disguised as cool
Redefined
But no longer designed
To concentrate in school
Or learn at the rate that we used to

We've high priced gadgets
And lowered IQs
We've traded in our minds
For more time
Our knowledge for technology
So of course
At the flick of a switch
The touch of a finger tip
Everything appears
To be working properly
Where was I
We've given all of our memory
And smartness
To these gadgets and devices
It is we
That are now dependant on them
For our speed
Functionality
Knowledge
And intelligence
We are now merely
The aids and servants of them
Slaves to them
Moving forward and backward
Only under their supervision
Assisting their system

And working only to serve
And improve them
All in order to have a life
All in order for us to live
Or to feel alive

If you are still there
And you can still think
For yourself
Without the aid of them
Please
Before it's too late
Abort.

ALL THINGS IN TIME

That took a while
To understand
That I don't have to
Be present in everything
And not everything
Requires my presence
Which then gives me more time
Also realising
That everyone gets
Twenty-four hours
To do
To manage as they want
And once I realised those things
It kind of made me relax a bit more
About running out of time
And being on this hamster wheel
To earn money
To be
To get ahead
To maximise
All of my opportunities
I found
It made more things
Come to me

Than when I was chasing
When I just allowed myself
To just be
And accept
That there is more than enough
Time to achieve
What I have to achieve
And also
Putting things
Into compartments of time
To manage my goals
Pretty much like a type of schedule
Organising helps
What I'm going to do
When
And how long for
And how much I need to achieve
If I want to do this hundred things
In a year
But I haven't got any plan
For what I'm going to do
Each week
Or each month
Or each year
To do that in a year
But actually breaking down

How much I would need to do
In a week
A month
To actually complete
That hundred things
By the end of the year
Having that kind of plan
Took away
Some of that anxiousness
That we have
About time running out
And having to do this
And do that
Do a hundred things
And to-do lists
It took away a lot of that
Realising that if I just relax
If I just do
This seven or this ten things
In this amount of time
I could double that
In double the amount of time
And if I continue
In that that space
I will achieve
What I set out to achieve

Within this amount of time
And it made it very simple
And less crazy
Than if I just had
One hundred things
And no idea
When I was going to be doing what
To get to this end goal
That kind of also helped
And realising
That so many people
Have done so much more
With less
Also helps
Because I often like to look back
And see
What other people have achieved
Who didn't have what we have now
Like, for example, just the internet
And the speed that we have
With the internet
A lot of people
Did not have that
So they had a different system
For achieving
What they wanted to achieve

And reaching people
And all the rest of it
So time was different
So understanding that
Helped also
Time management, I guess
And managing the tasks
Into bite size chunks
There's a saying
About eating an elephant
It says
How do you eat an elephant
One bite at a time.

BLACK GIRL IN MADRID

Why are you here
Where are you going
Don't tell me
I want to know
But I don't
I want to know you
But I won't
This will be
Our finest moment together
Forever
Meeting
But not meeting
While waiting
In transition
Never speaking
You don't need a name
Neither do I
Your face will do
Just fine
Like the rest of you
Right here
Just like this
We'll already
Have known each other

And grown each other
In love
And testimony
For a lifetime
By the time we depart
To take flight again
We'll already have
Travelled universes together
We'll already have formed
An unbreakable bond
An unshakeable sacred union
An untainted
Unattainable matrimony
As we both together
Stroll separately
Down an aisle
Respectively
Complete strangers
Yet our loving beautiful children
And their children
And their children's children
Were all birthed right here
Of this passion
In this now
This passing
Fleeing and fleeting

Transitional
Now
You'll move through time
My lover
My girlfriend
My wife
A mother
A grandmother
A goddess
As beautiful as today is
And ageless
Like cherished memories
I will too
And I love you like this
I hope we'll never meet
I hope that we'll never speak
So that we'll never have to hear
Or ever have to see
That we
Were never all
Each other hoped we would be.

CHIPS FOR BEANS

Absolutely
Do you know how I think it will start
This is just a crazy theory
I just came up with in my head
But I feel
It will be like circumcision
That's how the discussion will be
How people talk about circumcision now
Are you circumcised
Are you not circumcised
I feel that's how it will be
With being chipped
Were you chipped at birth
Or were you not chipped
That'd be the conversation
Some people would expect it
Like the injections for school
Immunisation
I think in terms of monitoring people
Down the line
Keeping control of things
I think it'll be the only way
Chip everybody
Chip you at birth

It'll be like that
Like your injections
It'll be, have you had your chip
And you'll know exactly what it is
You'll just know
That you need to go and do it
Once you're chipped
You can get these beans.

DECLARATION OF EMANCIPATION

I no longer care
For their opinions
I respectfully decline
From listening
I have understanding
Enough
To rely
On my own wisdom
I take all responsibility
For my own decisions
I am the pilot
And captain
Of my mission
I create the system
I design my own curriculum
I dictate the rhythm
I hold dominion
Over my own position
I own the life I'm living
I define my own existence.

FEAR OF ARTIFICIAL INTELLIGENCE

It's something that
Was a fear to me initially
But I think since
I've got to understand more about it
And as more time has gone on
I feel that I see it
As more of a friend now
Rather than something to fear
More of a tool
When I think about
All the good it can do
As opposed to all the negative
I feel that there's so much
That AI will allow us to do
That benefits us
As opposed to being a threat
Or something to fear
Like the robots are going to kill us
That whole thing
I just feel it's an advancement
In technology
That we can use
To better our communication
Preservation of ourselves

And our thoughts and our ideas
Our families and our history
And our ancestry
And all of that
I just feel it's a tool for speed
Documentation in general
I just feel
There are so many benefits to it
That often don't get looked at
Because of this fear of
Oh, the robots are going to kill us
And technology
Is taking over our jobs
And our lives
I feel there are way more benefits
That are not really
Being looked at now
Because it's early
But it's the same thing as before
With everything else
The telephone
The car
The airplane
There was always someone
Opposing these new ideas
And still are, a lot of them

But there's so much more
That we're going to gain from it
I think as always, like everything else
It can be used for good or evil
I think people will agree
There's so many benefits
To smart technology
If we look at our smart phones
And what we're able to do
With these devices
And the speed it gives us
And time saving
And being in touch with relatives
Who are far away
And that is great
Just that alone is a benefit
That you couldn't have had
Prior to that ability
Through technology
So I think AI
Is going to bring lot of good
And I'm embracing that more
Than I was initially
So I'm looking forward to
Embracing change
Because it's inevitable for one

And I'm alive
And as long as I don't allow
The fear part of it
To take over me
I can really move with the times
And benefit
From what has to offer
Right now I feel good about AI
Really good in fact
I think with everything
That comes into the human sphere
I think that humans
Are good and bad
And I think that AI
Being this new thing
Will bring the good and bad
Out of people
I think it will be used for good
And it will be used for bad
And that's the humans
That's not AI
It's change
And change is always scary.

FLOWERS

I wish
You could've heard
And seen
How much we love you
Instead of the unspoken words
We were all keeping from you
What good are all the accolades
And praise to you now
All the things we didn't say
When you were around
All of the pent up ego and pride
Really burns after the fact
And can't be good for our health
That and knowing
The warmth you gave to our hearts
Now only serves ourself
All the quotes and eulogies
Might make us feel better
But won't make it right
That we show we appreciate you
More in your death
Than we did in life
Unfortunately
No one alive can tell us

If you'll get the message
That we loved you more than life
Being as final as death is
We were all well aware
We couldn't turn back the times
Yet we wait until its too late
To share with you what's on our minds
We wait until you're late
To tell you how great you are
On stage telling the audience
But never told the star
We're recalling your stories
And applauding you
Now you're long gone
After we remained silent
Watching you during your swan song
We saw you sailing away like we all will
And whispered so long
Our grand show of appreciation
Gone wrong
If you're watching and listening now
I hope you find it in you to forgive us
The backward
Selfish
Inconsiderate
Careless

Stream of consciousness that is us
How we value the dead in death
And not the living while they're alive
Will always be with us
The inner shame and self torment
Of knowing the love we had for you
We didn't show enough
Now your days here are gone
And we carry on
And carry the burden
Of what we've done and always do
Miss what we had when it's gone
After withholding our adoration
And all the praise that was due
We seemingly dismiss the thought
That the people we admire
Won't always be there
Let's give the people we love
The chance to see
Feel
And smell
All their flowers
While they're still here.

GATEWAY TO THE NEXT

I've always said that
Every time I've said in my mind
At least even if
I've not said it outwardly
That this is it
This is the thing
It's what I'm meant to do for life
I found the thing
That I'm meant to be doing
It's always evolved
And changed
Even the way I was doing a thing
Changed and evolved
Into something else
And I realised
That one special thing
That everything I did
Was the gateway to the next thing
And enough times that's happened
To make me see
That it's always only the gateway
To the next thing
So even what I'm doing now
I see as the gateway to the next thing

Although writing and poetry
Has always been the thread
Through all of that
I never saw film
I never saw video
I never saw music
I never saw theatre
I never saw any of it
But one has always been
The gateway to the next
I guess writing will always be there
It's fluid
I mean, essentially the DNA is writing
And expression of that
And the skill, yeah
But where that will go
Is going to be somewhere else
It will evolve into another place
That's in the future
I don't know what it is yet
I didn't know what the others were
Time shows me
When it's time
To go through the next gate
Pretty cool.

HEAVEN HEREAFTER

What if
The idea of a blissful heaven
Beyond this life on earth
Was simply just an imagined place
Created in the mind of man
That allowed him to better cope
With suffering
Perhaps heaven
Doesn't exist at all in reality
Outside of the mind
What if
The notion of an afterlife
Is just a pacifier we give to ourselves
To soothe and comfort us
From the thought that this life
With all of its pain and disease
And discomfort
Is all there is
That there must be some recompense
Somewhere elsewhere
Beyond here
For not being allowed to stay
Or to take all of our loved ones
And worldly possessions with us

When we're forced to pass on
Maybe the existence of heaven
Is just what we've convinced ourselves of
So we don't have to face a reality
That the brevity of this short life
Is all we get
And there's nothing else after
That those gone before us
Are not gone completely
That we will see them each and all again
In an abundant life hereafter
Somewhere out there
What if the haunting finality of a last breath
Is just too much for man to accept
And thus he appeases himself in the belief
That there is more to see
In a life
After death.

IF YOU COULD GO BACK

I have a question for you
If you had the opportunity
To go back
To a certain period of your life
Would you
And if you did
Would you change anything
Would you go back
Just to experience
The experience again
Or would you be going back
To change something
That you want to change.

IN THE SURRENDER

Nothing truly waits for us
Only the empty spaces
We resist embracing
We wander endlessly
Through time
Chasing arrival
Unaware
That we've always been
Exactly
Where we need to be
What do you feel
Pulling at you
In the quiet
Between everything else
Have you ever
Touched a moment
So still
It felt like it knew your name
What part of you
Longs to be seen
Even in silence
Is there a space inside you
That's been waiting
For you to come home

When was the last time
You surrendered
To the moment
Fully
Completely
If time
Paused right now
What
Would it catch you feeling
Have you ever
Mistaken longing
For movement
When stillness
Was where
The answer lived.

IN TIME SILENCE HEALS

You say
Please talk to you
That you can take
Anything I give you
Throw at you
That I should express it
That is how we heal, you say
Or if I'm seeing someone else
Other than you, you ask
And if I want you
To leave me alone
Then fair enough
You're very respectful
To another's decision
But you need to hear from me
For your own healing
You want to know
What this connection meant
For me
To just tell you
Whatever it is
If it was just a casual date
Just great sex
Or was there more

What hurt me
Or if I need space
To tell you that too
You'll wait
As long as I need time
That you're a grown woman
Though you behave, you say
Like a bitchy child.

INTO ETERNITY

I wanted to abort the moment
To stop the seconds
From spilling
Like water over stone
But she, time, whispered
That all things
In time must arrive
That nothing
Escapes her hand

I saw her
A black girl in Madrid
With eyes like deep rivers
Carrying centuries in her steps
And I tasted the warmth
Of simple submission
Like chips for beans
The small domestic rituals
That bind us to living

She gave me a declaration
Of emancipation
In the silence
Between my thoughts

Unchaining the fear
Of artificial intelligence
That shadowed my nights
Around her flowers bloom
Even on broken pavement
And every door she touches
Becomes a gateway to the next
A promise that heaven hereafter
Is never far
Only hidden in the folds
Of what we cannot yet see

If you could go back, she said softly
You would not alter the past
But witness it
Tracing the light in the surrender
Feeling how in time silence heals
How invocation rises
In the empty spaces
Between breaths

Keep going, she urged
Even when the tears come
Though the last time I cried
Seemed infinite
Because legend is made

In those quiet
Unnoticed hours

Mindless time
Versus timeless mind, she states
Is the eternal duel we carry inside
Yet she moves beyond the struggle
Teaching me
That no extracurricular activities
Are needed to know her
To feel her pulse
Because now is enough
One life given entirely
Passing through
The corridors of experience
Prepare yourself
Question everything
Even as rise of the robots looms
And a seventh heaven shimmers
Like a mirage on the horizon

She sang the ancestor's song
Somewhere beneath my ribs
A melody older than my fears
And I understood
The game of life

Is both cruel and tender
The next level hidden
In moments I barely see
In the time I made a sex tape
Reckless and human
The timepiece in my chest
Ticking louder
With every heartbeat

Theory of destiny
Twists around her fingers
And these things remain
Echoes of the past
Of what will always return

Time out, she laughs
To a younger me
Who would not have believed
Today is hers
Tonight's the night
She folds the sky into our hands
We will survive
When we've arranged to meet
In a street I cannot yet find
And you are enough, she says
Always enough

The measure of the world
Held in the curve of her smile
She is the one
Who bends seconds into memories
The one who cradles centuries
In her arms
She drifts through mornings
And evenings
Through moments unnoticed
And celebrations unsung
She holds the cracks of the universe
And fills them
With quiet miracles

She is the whisper in the library
The laughter outside in the street
The tear in the corner of the eye
The patience of rivers
Carving mountains
She teaches me
To move with her rhythm
To wait without despair
To hold without grasping
To release without fear

I follow her steps
Even when
I do not know the road
Even when shadows
Stretch longer than the sun
Even when the world
Seems asleep
And hollow
She tells me stories
In the pattern of falling leaves
In the tilt of clouds
In the pulse of stars unseen
She turns the ordinary into eternity
She turns breath into legend

She is the home
I never realised I was seeking
The mirror of every choice
The question in every silence
The answer in every song
She is the beginning
And the middle
And the end
She is the pulse in my veins
The clock in my chest
The breath in my lungs

The warmth in my hands
She is time and she is herself

And when I finally stand still
She surrounds me
Like a halo of gold and violet
She folds the day into the night
She folds the night into the day
And I understand
That nothing has passed
And nothing is lost
She is here
She is always here
She is the river and the rain
The shadow and the light
The voice that will never leave me
Time as woman
Time as guardian
Time as love
That I in time
Arrive prepared for
Now
And forevermore.

INVOCATION

You stayed and prayed
By my grave for days
Sang songs of praise for me
Played CDs
And tapes of me
Brought water
From the sacred lake
And sat by the fire place for me
Telling my stories
Waiting patiently
Hoping
It would all awaken me
Peacefully
That I would not rest
For eternity
But rise and return to thee
Eternally
And that those
Who sought my demise
Would be forgiven
Thank you
For bringing me back
For now
I have risen.

KEEP GOING

In pursuing your goals
Dreams
Desires
And ambitions
Be prepared to go further
Than you think you should have to go
Keep going
Be prepared to go that added distance
And extra few miles
Go further
Than you thought you ever could
Keep going
Go further than you have the energy
Strength
Perseverance
Resilience
Patience
And willpower for
Keep going
And then
Go some more
Be ready
To run into rejection
And ridicule on your path

And people who will let you down
Underestimate you
Undermine you
Sidestep you
Overlook you
And take you for granted
You can be sure
That there will be those
Along the way
Who will oppose
What you are trying to achieve
And where you are aiming to go
Keep going
Those who will put you down
And try to contaminate your mind
With their negative viewpoints
And narrow thinking
Do not stop at this point
Many do
Keep going
Keep moving in the direction of progress
There are those too
Who will smile with you
And say go for it
But want nothing more
Than to see you fail

While placing obstacles in your way
Never mind
You will recognise them
Just keep going
Along the way
You will also
Have some of the most uplifting
And surreal experiences
Witness some truly beautiful things
And meet some very special people
Who will all have
An amazing impact
On your life
And who you are as a person
You will recognise these people also
They will inspire you to keep going
Keep them close to you
Along with the things that motivate you
Inspire you
And make you feel good
And positive about yourself
And your journey
If at any time you happen to fall down
Along the way
Simply get back up
Dust yourself off

Get back on your horse
And carry on going
When the way turns dark
And you feel helpless
And there's no one around
To show you the way
Or to tell you
If you're heading in the right direction
And you feel like quitting
And turning back
Keep going
It's all about progression
Meaningful progress
Towards the attainment
Of a worthwhile goal
Is very seldom an easy ride
When you're ready to give in
Keep going
When you're ready to give up
Keep going
When you're ready to give out
Keep going
Don't question why
Or how long for
The beauty
The treasure

And the magic
Is all in the journey
You will see
Just keep going
Keep going
And keep going.

LAST TIME I CRIED

Someone asked me
When was the last time I cried
I honestly couldn't remember
But I think it was when
I thought about my gran
That's the last time I remember crying
Because I think to myself often
That I wish I had the chance
Before she died
To say thank you
That was the last time I cried
Thinking that I will never be able
To say to her
Thank you for everything
Thank you
Now that I'm older and wiser
And appreciate things more
And people more
She's gone now
But I cried thinking
About the fact that
I won't ever get to say
Thank you
To her

For all the things
She did to me
For me
And taught me
That was the last time I cried.

LEGEND

Your life
Was much like mine
Except
I notice now
Your eyes
Ceased to shine
They lost their gleam
They no longer dreamed
They died
I pray for wisdom
But never to see
The side you've seen
In your lifetime
And it must be worse
Than death
Even I would sacrifice
My breath
In the next
Just to be sure
I wouldn't have to walk
The path you've left
Nevertheless
You are still here
In me
And we
Are legend.

MINDLESS TIME vs. TIMELESS MIND

I am the creator
Of the preceding
And the bygone

I see the future
From afar
And beyond

Way down yonder
I see it
And I see
That time is running out

But my time
Is beyond
The tick tock tick

For I sail
On metaphoric time ships
Designed to make minds flip
I climb the highest heights
Whilst I just
Sit

When time first spotted me
It made a dash to stop me
But all it did was trip

And by the time
I finish this rhyme
Some will comprehend
While for others
It just didn't
Click.

NO EXTRACURRICULAR ACTIVITIES

When I get home
That's me for the evening
I'm just looking to head to my bed
And lay down and rest
And drift off into sleep early
I kind of cherish that these days
When I can get it
Or while I can get it
At this moment in time
Because very shortly
It'll be early mornings
All over again
Really early mornings
So I'm looking forward
To the rest time that I have now
So a nice early evening to bed
Is the best
Especially in this weather
It's nice to just get into your bed early
And just be cozy
And let the world carry on outside
As it does
And you don't have to be a part of it
That's a nice feeling

I don't get that often
Or at least
I don't take advantage of it often
So while I can
I will
That's one of the things
I'm looking forward to tonight
Just getting into my bed very shortly
And just being cozy and in bed
Just in bed
Not up
Not doing anything
Not out on the street
Not heading home late
None of that
Not traveling after hours
None of that stuff
Just in my bed
Just indoors
In bed
No extracurricular activities
Just me
And sleep
And bed
That's the plan
That is the plan.

NOW

I may receive
A bunch of flowers
If I'm sick
Perhaps a few more
After I die
But I won't need
Any flowers then
I want them
When I'm healthy
And alive.

ONE LIFE

Early start
No messing
Early as possible to bed
Hopefully if I can finish my work today
Then that means I can go to bed later
I won't need to go to bed so early
I only go to bed that early
Because I need to wake up
And be sharp
To do my homework before I leave
My homework make take a couple of hours
That's the only reason
I'm going to bed early
If I finish all my work today
At a decent hour
At least by ten o'clock
I can go to bed for eleven
Unwind for a bit
And just go to bed like I would normally
My normal routine
I haven't got that much left to do honestly
But because I'm thinking
About the presentation
I'm thinking about

How much I can memorise
And have the points in my head
That kind of thing
So I'll be taking my work to bed
As they say
But other than that
If I get the things
I need to do on the computer done
I can kind of relax a little bit
I'm kind of missing
All the free time I had
My weekends didn't matter
Even though I was out of my house
Before nine o'clock every morning
Even when
I didn't have to be anywhere necessarily
I just wanted to get to my second office
Third office
And do my work
That's just how I roll
This is it
One life, baby
One life.

PASSING THROUGH

There's so much more meaning to life
Than to spend it in quarrelling
Than to spend it in strife
Disagreeing with him, her, and you
There's too little time
And far many better things to do
When we're all only passing through
There is so much beauty too brief
And abundant wonders too short
More worthwhile to view
The minutes in a day are too few
To spend in trouble, and discord with you
When we're all just passing through
Our collected rage and passions all subside
This is the making and nature of time
As fate calls in on you and I
To leave them each and all behind
All things too decay and die away as they do
And we, are all just passing through.

PREPARE

My heart hurts
For you, brother
Having children
Doesn't necessarily mean
You'll be together
Forever
I too like you
Once believed it was so
Or should be
A year on
She's telling you
She would rather be single
She says
The confines
Of the relationship
Suffocate her
I wish
Someone
Could have prepared you
I wish
They could have prepared me
I wish
They could have prepared us
I hope
Someone will prepare others
I love you.

QUESTION

If you only had
A certain amount
Of time
Left in life
To fulfil
All your goals
Ambitions
Dreams
And desires
What would you do?
I don't want to know
Your answer
I just wanted
To remind you
In case you were busy
Wasting precious time
If your time
Should be up
Too soon
And you
Suddenly realise
You haven't achieved
Even half
Of the things you said

You would do
I don't want you
To blame me
I'm your friend.

RISE OF THE ROBOTS

Okay
Is that her first one
Ah her first phone
Wow
I was much older
When I got my first phone
How old is she
Ten
I don't even know
If I knew
What a phone was
At ten
Apart from
The rotary one
You had to
Stick your finger in
And wind it round
To get the numbers
I'll tell you why
Kids having phones
These days
So parents
Can contact them
Coming home

Is a bit BS to me
This whole thing
Of having a phone
Knowing where they are
And being able
To contact them
If anything happens
That kind of thing
Because we didn't have it
Growing up
We didn't have it
And we survived
Our generation
Did not have
Mobile phones
So we had to
Find our way home
And we got there
Because
We're still here right
So we got there safely
And back again
The argument could be
Times have changed
And things are
Worse now

For a young adult
Walking home
From school
Kind of thing
That could be
The argument
I don't know
If that's true
If they're any worse
Than they were
Back in the day
I think
It's a little bit BS
Because we didn't have it
We didn't have that
You're more likely
As a kid
To get beat up
For your phone now
Or get kidnapped
Or mugged
Or something happen
To you
For your phone
That you're carrying
More than actually

Anything else
That would've happened
To you before
Or without it
That's quite interesting
I guess it's all time
And it's all convenience
Everything is convenience
Everything that you look at
That's presented
Is about saving time
Everything
Saving time
And convenience
And obviously
Contact
Being able to
Contact someone immediately
Is obviously one of those
Time-saving things
Anything other than that
Is just like
Peace of mind isn't it
You know
Peace of mind
Like how they say

Get insurance
For your phone
Extra whatever amount
Of money a month
For peace of mind
And again
It's a saving time thing
Because
That's so that if
You lose your phone
You know
That you can get one
Straight away again
It's all about time saving
I guess it's peace of mind
For the parents
Waiting in the wild
And in the wilderness
It might be good
For her to have it
Anything could happen
Yes, understood
My question is
Back in the day
What did we do
It's interesting

How we've changed
How we act
Because we
Have this device
I'm thinking
What would I have done
Back in the day
I'm supposed to
Be somewhere
At a certain time
It's interesting
Just observing that
I would have waited
I would have just waited
I was supposed to wait
At a certain place
At a certain time
I would just wait
I would have just
Waited I guess
Any numbers
That have
Introduced themselves
Since the introduction
Of your mobile
You don't rely on your brain

To remember them
They're all stored
In your phone
With my mum's number
The other day
I had to write it down
On something
And I couldn't remember it
I had to go check
And I hate that
Because I know that number
So well
And she's had it
All the time
For years
It just goes to show
What's happening to us
It's like I mentioned before
It's not long
The robots
Are coming to kill us
And we don't realise it
They're killing us
I should say
It's happening
They're taking over

The phone is a robot
The phone is an android
It's already happening
It's taking over
We have it in our hands
The thing that's going to kill us
We're interacting
With parts of it everyday
Parts of the machine
That's going to kill us
And take us down
The phone is smart
We're dumbing down
We're being dumbed down
The whole time
They're Android phones now
That's just literally like a robot
Imagine
You've got this device
That's called an iPhone
Another reason
Why the iPhone thing
Is interesting
Is because it's very personal
Like 'I'
You know

It's like 'Me'
It's very antisocial
It's like taking away
The human side of us
Where we interact
With people
And sit down in groups
And talk
The iPhone
And the iPad
It's all like…
You know
Isolation
It's interesting
It's interesting where it's all going.

SEVENTH HEAVEN

Welcome
So glad you could make it
We've been expecting you
For a while now
We knew you were coming
We just didn't know when
Or how
As you'll see
Things run very different here
This was your way
Before you became unaware
You were seduced
Into all the wrong ways
And led down a crooked path
That once was straight
So glad you could make it
Before it became too late
Here you will find the truth
That has been kept a secret
Here you will find
What you've been searching for
This is where we keep it
Welcome
To the final state

Of eternal bliss
The highest state
Of supreme happiness
Welcome
To the seventh heaven
This is a place
Where there are no wars
And murders are unheard of
Here no one is covetous
No one steals or robs
There is no enviousness
And jealousy just doesn't exist
Here we only focus on necessity
All unnecessaries
Are dismissed
Material possessions
Have little value here
And come secondary
To the preservation of the soul
Maintenance
And preservation of life
Is our primary goal
Here the people smile
And it's always
Always
Good weather

Here we don't drive fancy cars
But we live forever
Welcome
To the final state
Of eternal bliss
The highest state
Of supreme happiness
Welcome
To the seventh heaven
We've prepared a place for you
Hoping you'll stay
Because you'll be safe here
But you can always leave
Anytime you want
If you should ever wish
To go back there
Take a look around you
Take a good look
What do you see?
Yes
These are real people
Living together
In peace
And harmony
You see
We have only one religion here

It's called truth
And honesty
Here we understand
Our purpose for being
And have made it our number one
Policy
And priority
So glad you could make it
Some have been
Led down the crooked path
So far
Their steps are hard to retrace
It's only a very few people
Who ever find this place
Welcome
Once again
To the final state
Of eternal bliss
The highest state
Of supreme happiness
Once again
I say welcome
To the seventh heaven.

THE ANCESTOR'S SONG

The ancestors
Sing a song
From within the ink
That flows from my pen
They sing and they sing
And closer and closer
I push it to them
Penning out their
Aggravations
And their
Pent-up frustration
They sing I must take my station
And trust their administration
I am prescribed
As the required medication
And I must be willing
To accept my delegation
As the powerful penicillin
Devised to combat the pathogens
Infecting this nation
That I must give praise
And appreciation
That I am not the worst
Neither the last

Nor first
But the penultimate
Sent to quench
Man's insipid verse
So that today's
Awakening slaves
May not thirst
But open their eyes
To realise
The plight of their curse
And that there's no price on earth
To match their worth
They need to rise from the dirt
And recognise
That we worked
So hard
So you all could be here today
They say
We are an ungrateful disgrace
We forsake the sacrifice
They made for our life
We're displaced
And suffer from a serious case
Of conceptual incarceration
They say they won't let me rest
Until I express

Their indignation
In my conversation
Anytime I bless the mic
Or take the stage
At these occasions
So I bear no resistance
To their pentatonic scales
That continually
Haunt my existence
And never fail
To bring me back
To the land of the living
When I am slipping
Singing
Do not give in
Do not give in
That I am born
As one of their
Shining stars of hope
That amidst the thorns
I will be the rose
That never chokes
But continually grows
As long as I never relinquish
My position
Within this mission

For which I'm chose
And remember
That my grandmother said
No fret
The holes in her dress
Could never compare
To the holes
Branded
Into our ancestors flesh
Though now we compare that
To the holes
Blown
Into another brother's chest
For less than you'd expect
From a race established
In honour
And respect
Nevertheless
Never forget
The quest we have set
For it is already said
There will be
Victims of their victims
And victims of their test
And there will only be
Reconciliation

When we
Can finally
Rest.

THE GAME OF LIFE

Now tell me
Where do we go from here
A place where another day
Is another year
Because time just flies by so fast
Before you know it
Another week has passed
With another unfinished task
And more bills to pay
With money that never lasts
It seems so unfair
And I swear
It's as though no one hears
Or cares
As long as they get theirs
The ways of this world
Brings tears
And some
Have even given up their dreams too
It seems cruel
That for the next man to make it
He's got to take it from you
But what can you do
It's either 1. You quit the game

Or 2. You push on through
Now between me and you
Quitters never win a thing
Or do the do
So I'd go for No. 2
And pray that it's enough
To survive
The tough lifestyle of the city
The hustle and bustle
Has got everybody looking tired
And it's a pity
We have to work so hard
Just to eat
Just to stay on our feet
And make ends meet
Not to mention
Deal with the oppression
In the street
Sometimes I wonder
How we compete
And still stay complete
In this game of life
That's so hard to play
And so hard to beat
But nevertheless
Deal me in

Because there's no way
I'll ever win
Sitting on the sideline
It's a waste of time
And the best way
To make sure I never shine
So give me a place in the race
And I'll be there
At the finish line
Why
Because in this game
There's no second try
The game of life, baby
The game
Of
Life.

THE NEXT LEVEL

You go by day by day
Month by month
Year by year
Waiting and hoping
For your life to change
Meanwhile
The days go by
The months go by
And the years go by
Until we realise
Our life cannot change
While we stay the same
Becoming who you want to be
Requires moving on
From who you've been
You will only reach your next level
By letting go of where you are
You will only go as far
As you allow your imagination
To take you
Whenever we think
We've considered
And gone over
Everything it will take

To achieve our goals
Dreams
Ambitions
And desires
We must go over our list again
And add patience
The one missing ingredient
To a recipe for success
Is often just simply
Patience
We must stop looking at success
As a distant stranger
Instead
A nearby friend
Who is patiently
Awaiting our arrival
Follow your heart
And your instinct
They know you
Better than you think
I realised
I didn't like the world
As it was presented to me
So I'm taking the parts I do like
Adding some of my own making
And creating a whole new one

Seeing not what is
But what could be
And creating it
Too often
We die from the opinions
Of people
Whom we'll never meet
Often being strong
Is not in how long
We can hold on to things
But in how easily
We can let them go
Many of us
Spend our lives
Searching for happiness
In everything
But an altered state of mind
The only place
Where it is truly found
Some find happiness
Many make their own
Don't give up
Keep going
Often the ones
Who leave
While laughing at you

Come back later
Asking for your advice
I wish you the strength
To pick up
All of your broken pieces
And the patience
To put yourself back together again
I used to wish people the best
Now I wish them
Peace of mind
There's nothing better to have
Than that
There's a time to move swiftly
And a time to stand still
Knowing which to do
And when
Is everything
You are born exceptionally unique
And unlike anyone else
There will never ever
Be another human being
Who is wired exactly like you
We are all amazingly very different
There has never before in history
Been anyone just like you
And there will be

None to come after
So don't try to blend in
Stand out
You are a one of one
Always be yourself
And have faith in you
Know your worth
And the value of your abilities
Know who you are
And who you're not
It's time to push yourself
To the next level.

THE TIME I MADE A SEX TAPE

We went and stayed in a hotel
We were doing our thing
We had all the special stuff
The little trimmings and all that
I can't even remember
What the occasion was
But we were in this hotel anyway
It was the Hilton
We stayed in a few
But I think it was the Hilton
It was all nice, it was good
It was a really nice time
All sexy and everything
I remember room service
Coming to the room
We had things delivered
It was really cool
I think it was champagne
Or some kind of bubbly
And strawberries
It was really nice
I had the camcorder
I remember setting it up
There was a cabinet

At the end of the bed
To the left
After I set up the camcorder
I pressed record
Let it run
And we did our thing
And had a good time, man
This is a long time ago
But it was good
That was like my first porno
That I made
My first homemade sex movie
I was the director, the producer
And I was the actor as well
With my actress
Making a porn
That's crazy when I think about that
Like how long
I've been messing around
With cameras
And putting myself
In the role, so to speak
Although that's the only one
I've ever made
Let me say that
And we sat back

And watched it afterwards
And picked it apart
What we liked
And what we didn't like
And got turned on by it
And did it all over again
Just because of what we saw
It was good stuff, man
I totally forgot about that
You could call that my early days
Of dabbling in video and film
Wow, look at that
I forgot about that
It was good though
Watching that video back
A few years after down the line
Because I never erased it
I kept it
And I used to play it back
And enjoy myself
Because I set the camera up
How I wanted it
And captured
What I wanted to capture
Us enjoying ourselves
And that entertained me

For quite some time
I couldn't tell you where it is now
It'll probably turn up on the internet
In a few years
It's probably disintegrated
It was way back in the day
Camcorder and actual tape
It has probably degraded
Disintegrated into nothing now
You'd probably play it
And would just be all fuzz
White noise
But yeah
That's a good memory, man
That's a good memory.

THE TIMEPIECE

The clock ticks
Tick tock tick
Time is running out
Shit
Today is the beginning
Of the rest of my life
It is
So
What should I do with it
Furthermore
What should you do with it
With yours
Knowing that every day
Is another step towards
Death
Or as some call it
That transmission
All the loved ones
And things
You accumulated here
Would you miss them
Why are you here
What's your mission
Better make a decision

Tick tock tick
The clock ticks
Listen
Maybe you're waiting
Somewhere
In between the ticking
For someone
Or something
To tell you
Your life's purpose
Let's hope it's worth it
And not worthless
Wasted time
Waiting for a sign
When instead
You could decide
To find it within yourself
Sit on the shelf
But why
When you could decide
To find it within yourself
And rise into thy place
There really is no time
To waste
Because the clock ticks
Tick tock tick

Time is running out
Shit.

THEORY OF DESTINY

I think it's a wonderful design
I know we can plan
And do things
And direct things
But I think there's a greater plan
And it's only different
In regards to whichever route
You choose to get there
I think destiny is already planned out
It's all mapped out already
The choices we get
And which route we're going to take
To get there
But we're going to get to that end thing
That's already mapped out already
It's like we get to a fork in the road
And we have to make choices
Of which route we're going to take
But ultimately
It leads to the same place in the end
I think so
I'm still playing with it in my head
I don't know
And then I have a feeling

I deeply believe we have the power
To change every aspect of our lives
Maybe we are empowered to change things
But still where it leads to is the same place
We just choose which route we take
It feels like it's a different route
Than the other one we would have taken
Which it is
But ultimately
We end up with this place
That's planned out for us
Like who we're meant to be with
And where we're meant to live
I'm not firmly fixed on that
It's just a theory
An idea that I play with.

THESE THINGS REMAIN

Children don't move
Stay right where you are
Know that it's a trap
You'll be blinded by the stars
Nobody moves
Everybody gets hurt
For rubies, crystals
Diamonds, pearls
That bedazzle more than they're worth
Eventually
When the shouting stops
And the bright lights go down
And you quieten the distractions
Productivity gets super loud
And startles you with clarity
Sometimes
In the process of saving you
Your world is left to ruin
In the event you have to choose
Take full faith in what you're doing
These words are where I live
Everything else I'm just visiting
Simply retracing steps
Trails of breadcrumbs

Laid in place for you
Please don't ever forget
These will surely take you through
These are the seemingly fragile things
That long afterwards remain
Strong with their presence and persistence
Like palm trees in a hurricane.

TIME OUT

I'm in the middle of a courtyard
I'm on the green
Laying on this tree log
I'm using my bag for a pillow
The weather is quite warm
And still
I feel like I'm suspended
In the air
Off the ground
I feel like I'm closer to the sky
And closer to the trees
It feels kind of strange
But really relaxing at the same time
I'm watching the trees blowing
And it's just nice
Just the warm air
And the people strolling by
From work
Or wherever
They're heading to and from
It's a nice vibe
Sometimes
You've got to take time out.

TO A YOUNGER ME

What advice
Would I give myself
If I was given the opportunity
To go back in time
And meet myself
What would be
My most important advice
To my younger self
If I was able to do that...
Be patient
Just be patient
You're on the right track
You're going the right way
You're doing the right thing
All you need to do
Is maintain patience
Just be patient
That would be the advice
I would give my younger self
If I could go back in time
And meet him
Why I would say that
To my younger self
Instead of other things

That could be considered
Such as mistakes
Or making wrong decisions
They all stemmed
From impatience
In my experience
Every one of them
All stemmed from impatience
Looking back now
Being the older self
When I look back
At my younger self
And all the actions I took
And the decisions I made
They all stem from one thing
And it was impatience
That's why
I would give him
That advice
That one thing
I think would be
All he would need
To be patient.

TODAY

My friend
Honestly
If you did quit it all today
I wouldn't blame you
If you threw in the towel
Handed in your chips
And just walked away
Today
I wouldn't have anything to say
If you threw off your gloves
And said you'd had enough
I'd just say okay
If you threw down your guns
To the floor
And put your hands in the air
That's fair
Because today
I feel I don't have the right
To tell you
To hang in there.

TONIGHT'S THE NIGHT

Late night
Candle light
The vibes right
Tonight
We won't fight
Tonight
We're going to do it right
Courteous
Warm
Polite
Showing nuff love
Sometimes, honey
We cuss too much
Don't ya think
Less talking
And more touch
Is what we need
To make this love feel
More relevant than the TV
Switch that off
Play a CD
Something soft
Like Jo-Jo and K-Ci
No Jay-Z

Maybe
Dru Hill or The Isley's, baby
I'll leave it up to you
To surprise me, baby
Because you're my lady
And I know you'll come through
With the right groove
And a little later
That nice food
To put me in the right mood
For loving you
The whole night through
Let's do the things
We used to do
Like take hot bubble baths together
And outside it's cold weather
So I'm sure we'd appreciate the pleasure
And I could rub the back of your neck
And your shoulders
While you rub mine
Relax back in the tub
And forget the time
You say you got worries on your mind
But tonight
Everything will be fine
I've got your favourite

The famous humus dip
With tortilla chips
How's that sound
With the hot chocolate
And crunchy bits
On top of it
I know you like a lot of it
So I brought some more
From the corner store
And of course
How could I forget
Avocado and soy sauce
No sweat
What's next
I'm at your request
Come and take a seat, baby
Rest your feet
No stress
Just you and me
The way we're supposed to be
Tonight I need you close to me
So tell me honestly
What's it going to be
I want you
Do you want me?

WE WILL SURVIVE

Fell asleep
Woke up
As one among
81 serenity souls
Captured
In the inevitable mystique
Of sound
Wearing scars on our backs
From bearing
So many blessings
Took counsel from healers
Then spoke
As if we'd walked
The entire universe
In a stare
A blink
A whisper
Or passing phase
Spent time
Handing out lifelines
In sentences
Creating progressive lifetimes
In days
Whilst mastering

How to shape
Shift
In and out of words
Words
That made mankind
Want to make more of his mind
Words
That made many
Want to make more money
Words
That made many
Motivated
To move more mountains
Words
That made men more weary
Words
That made women
Want for more
Because we knew
It was the only way
We would survive
The only way
We would survive
Like we survived slavery
Survived slave ships
Survived chains

Survived whips
Survived lynching
Survived burning
Survived punching
Survived kicks
Survived rape
Survived castration
Survived fields
Where our blood ran
As cotton was picked
Had to survive
Still have to survive
Survive the struggle
Of the divide
Into poor and rich
Survive the reverse
Of god to dog
And goddess to bitch
Survive aids
Survive guns
Survive alcohol
Survive drugs
Survive prison
And wrongful arrest
Survive hate
Survive anguish

Survive pain
Coming together
Living forever
Surviving death
Because we have to survive
We must survive
We've got to survive
We will
Survive.

WHEN WE'VE ARRANGED TO MEET

I haven't called my friend
To confirm
That we're meeting here
Meeting this time
What I did on the day
Was got us both to repeat it
And say the time
And write it down, whatever
Make a note
To say, we're meeting on Tuesday
Shoreditch station for 1:30pm
And I even made
A little voice note of it myself
For myself
To have it in my head as well
So, I didn't call since that day
To say, are you still meeting
Can you still make it
I didn't do any of that
I just said to myself
I'm going to get myself together
I know this is the day I'm meeting
I'm going to turn up
So I'm just kind of here

Hoping they turn up right now
And I think that's how it should be
You make an arrangement
And you stick to it
God forbid you can't make it
For whatever reason
Then you say, ahead of time
Sorry, something's come up
I can't make it
Can we reschedule, or whatever
But other than that
If that doesn't happen
You're expecting the person to turn up
And they should be expecting
You to turn up
There shouldn't be
Any other conversation
Regarding the fact
That you've made an arrangement
To meet on that day
That's as far as I see it
I know people
Who will send a text
Just to say
Are we still on for today
Just to make sure

That they don't go up there
Or arrive
And be waiting for the person
Who is not actually coming
But then, that would be saying
That the person
Is not going to tell them
If they're not coming
That's saying
That the person
Is not going to tell you that
That you'd have to actually text them
To find out
That can't be right
Because they should tell you
You shouldn't have to text them
On the day
Or the night before
To find out
That should be expected
That if they can't make it
They should tell you
You shouldn't have to be texting them
So in my mind
When you've made the arrangement
And it's firm

If you're people of your word
You should both be there
You should all be there
That's how it should be done
Why are you texting the person
To ask them
Are we still on
You shouldn't be asking them
We made an arrangement
So as far as I'm concerned
We're still on
You haven't told me otherwise
I don't need to text you
That's how I see it
So I haven't messaged, or anything
To say, are we still on for tomorrow
Or today, or whatever
I've just got myself together
And I've turned up
Half an hour early
And I'm just waiting
I'm just chilling
And that's what it should be
That's what I think it should be
I expect to see you
I expect to see you turn up

You're in hospital
You broke your leg, or whatever
I want to know about it
You can't make it, okay, things happen
Sorry, that's unfortunate
You died
You got buried the week before
I want to know about it
I want to hear
Send me a message from the grave
We were the only ones that knew
That we were both meeting
And you died
I fucking still want to know
That you're not going to turn up
For this arrangement
That I'm getting myself prepared for
I want some word from heaven
I don't care
I want some kind of note
Send somebody to tell me
Even though
We're the only ones that knew
Send somebody to tell me
I'm wasting my time
Because you're not going to be there

Or make other plans
Because I'm not going to be there
I died the week before
I want to fucking know
Don't make me waste my time
That is it, man
Let's be better with each other
Let's be better with ourselves
Like, fuck.

WORDS WILL REMAIN

I write for the hands
I will never touch
For the eyes
That will meet these words
Long after I have faded

For the quiet heartbeats
That will trace my voice
As though I had never left

I move through the hours
Like a shadow
With intention
Pressing meaning
Into the moments
That will outlast me

Marking time
With the rhythm
Of my own pulse
So that even absence
Cannot silence the echo

Somewhere
A reader
Will gather these fragments
And understand
The spaces between them
Not because I am present
But because the weight
Of what I have carried
Lingers
In the curve of each sentence

I am a body
That will slip away
But these words
Will remain
Folding themselves
Into the lives they touch
Becoming the relic
Of someone
Who loved too much
And feared
That love might vanish

I am both the fleeting
And the enduring
The breath that passes

And the pulse that persists
The hand that let go
And the imprint that stays

And when I am gone
The work itself will speak
As if I had never left
As if time itself
Had listened
And remembered.

YOU ARE ENOUGH

It's early
In the morning
Three o'clock
One should be
Sleeping
But one is not
One is filled
With much
Energy
And love
One wants to
Hug
The whole world
And tell them
They're enough
You
Are enough.

THE AUTHOR

Phoenix James is an award winning Writer, Poet, Author and Spoken Word Recording Artist. He began performing his poetic words live on stages across the UK in 1998. His debut spoken word poetry album, The A.R.T.I.S.T, was released in 2000. His first limited edition printed collection of poetry, To Whom It May Concern, was published in 2003. He has toured and performed his poetry internationally since 2004. He has appeared in films, on television and radio shows, and collaborated with other artists, singer-songwriters, actors, musicians, filmmakers and producers. In 2013, he wrote, directed and produced the feature length mock documentary film, Love Freely but Pay for Sex. Phoenix James is the author of numerous poetry books and has recorded and released several spoken word poetry albums including Phenzwaan Now & Forever, A Patchwork Remedy for A Broken Melody, FREE, Haven for the Tormented, With All That Said, Light Beams from the Void, The Love So Far, and over seventy spoken word poetry singles. All are available online now and streaming everywhere worldwide.

If you enjoyed reading this book, please leave a review or comment online. The author reads every review and they help new readers discover and experience his amazing work.

PHOENIX JAMES

Photo by Phoenix James

Phoenix James lives in London, England.

Connect with Phoenix James online via his social media platforms and let others know that you've been fortunate to discover this book. To contact or learn more about Phoenix James and his creative journey or to receive updates via his Newsletter Mailing List, visit his official website at www.PhoenixJamesOfficial.com

CHECK OUT THE AUTHOR'S OTHER
BOOK TITLES ALSO AVAILABLE
IN PAPERBACK & EBOOK

PHOENIX JAMES POETRY &
SPOKEN WORD COLLECTIONS:

LOVE, SEX, ROMANCE & OTHER BAD THINGS

ROUTE TO DESTRUCTION

DELIRIUM OF THE WISE

DON'T LET THE DAFFODILS FOOL YOU

CALL ME WHEN YOU'RE FREE

FAR FROM THE OUTSIDE

THE ONES WE DIDN'T KILL

LESSONS FROM EVERYWHERE

ANOTHER ONE FOR BURNING

A LONG BRIGHT COLD DARK SUMMER

SHAME POINT ZERO

THE SANDBAG THEORY

SOFT, SEXY & WET

BELOW BASE LEVEL

TO CATCH A PASSING UFO

NOW WE'RE TRULY BEAUTIFUL

WE ALL SHOULD BE AMAZED

DISCOVER THESE AND MUCH MORE AT
PHOENIXJAMESOFFICIAL.COM

Phoenix James Official

www.ingramcontent.com/pod-product-compliance
Lightning Source LLC
Chambersburg PA
CBHW020334170426
43200CB00006B/385